Claude Monet's immense
body of work is
spread among
many museums and
private collections.
Visitors to Giverny
can find a presentation
of them in a number of
different works,
especially *Hommage à
Claude Monet*, published
in the spring of 1980 for
one of France's most
prestigious exhibitions,
held at the
Grand Palais in Paris.
To introduce
readers to the great
painter's mansion,
gardens and
everyday world,
photographs
are the illustrations used,
in an approach
guided by the humble
hope that Monet, himself
a fervent photographer,
would have approved.

Previous page:
Claude Monet

A VISIT TO
GIVERNY

GERALD VAN DER KEMP

THE LIFE OF MONET

Giverny! A charming village spread out along a hillside not far from Vernon... Giverny, a name now famous because of the residence chosen by a great artist. It was there that Claude Monet decided to settle in April 1883. "I am filled with delight, Giverny is a splendid spot for me...", he wrote, scarcely one month after moving there. Before visiting his home, his garden and his ponds, one should say something of the painter's life and his sources of inspiration.

Claude Monet came into the world in Paris in 1840. He spent his childhood and youth at Le Havre where, in the years between 1858 and 1862, he met the painters Eugène Boudin and Jongkind, who introduced him to the pleasures of painting in the open air, directly from nature. While studying in Paris, he met Renoir, Sisley and Bazille. He admired Manet and worked side by side with Courbet at Trouville. In London in 1871, he discovered Turner and it was at this time that he began to admire and collect Japanese engravings. He settled in Argenteuil between 1872 and 1878 and began to work on the water in a boat converted into a studio. He suffered a period of extreme hardship during these years. He married Camille who bore him a son, Jean. His works were exhibited in 1874, 1876, 1877 and 1882, alongside works by painters who were to be known as "impressionists", after an 1872 painting which Monet had entitled "Impression, soleil levant".

In 1876, Ernest Hoschedé, a businessman and collector, invited him to the château of Rottembourg in Montgeron. He became a family friend and met Edouard Manet,

"It is essential to go on a pilgrimage to the flower-bedecked sanctuary of Giverny to understand Monet more deeply, to better grasp his sources of inspiration and to imagine that he is still living among us."
VAN DER KEMP

Carolus-Duran and many others there. Ernest Hoschedé went bankrupt and fled to Belgium in 1877. Madame Hoschedé and Madame Monet decided to spend the summer of 1878 together. They rented a house in Vétheuil but Claude Monet was completely lacking in enthusiasm about it.

His wife gave birth to a second son, Michel, and she herself died of tuberculosis in 1879, a painful loss for Monet. Alice Hoschedé then decided to help Claude by bringing up his two children together with her own. They left for Poissy, which Monet hated and, when the lease was up in April 1883, he visited the outer areas of Vexin in search of other accomodation. From the doorway of the little train between Vernon and Gasny he discovered Giverny, where he moved with Alice Hoschedé and the children. To begin with they lived in an inn and then

Today visitors can see the dazzling palette that the master of Giverny wanted to compose just a few steps from his house.

There is no longer any need to know how he created his garden. It is clear that he created it following the successive order of his eyes' commands, according to each day's invitations, to satisfy his appetite for colors.
CLEMENCEAU

Subjective rendering is
what is sought by a new
use of colors whose
aim is to place th
most importance on
light. The colors are
painted pure
on the canvas rather than
mixed on the palette.
The personal impression,
rather than the objective
expression of a subject,
must dominate.
GUILLAUD

rented a house from Louis-Joseph Singeot. It was here that Claude Monet settled permanently. The property spread over almost two and a half acres and sloped down towards the bottom of the village. At the lower end is the "chemin du Roy", along which ran a small local railway connecting Vernon and Gasny, and at the upper limit was the "rue de l'Amsicourt", now called the "rue Claude Monet" (where you will find the entrance to the Foundation, in front of the car park). The house stands beside the road and looks onto a large orchard. There is a single-storey barn to the left of the house as one comes from the garden. Monet immediately made this his drawing room and studio, where he loved to sit and smoke while examining in minute detail the canvases painted in the open air.

He had flowers planted in his garden to enable him to paint in either fine or rainy weather. Every day, untiringly, he reproduced on his canvases the fields, the trees and the river Seine. He even bought an island for this purpose, the "île aux Orties", on which he owned a hut and a boat-studio. The painter Helleu's daughter, Paulette Howard Johnston, describes him as being "of medium height, stout, with a thick neck and standing squarely on his legs, his hair cut very close with, however, a very long white beard. He wore a suit of a thick, greyish woollen fabric, trousers fastened at the ankles, a white shirt with finely folded cuffs which just showed under the sleeves of his high-buttoned jacket... He had a clear, ringing voice... he was extremely simple and natural; his direct way of

speaking inspired confidence and although he gave the impression at first sight of being rather peasant-like, this vanished as soon as he began to speak : one quickly realized just how refined his mind was". Lucien Descaves noted that he liked good living, drinking his wine pure, and could bear water only in small doses after his morning drink of chocolate. However, he smoked forty cigarettes a day... mostly in the open air and threw them away half-smoked. He always had several canvases underway due to

Claude Monet's passion for flowers can be fully understood by visiting his garden, which his contemporaries described as one of his masterpieces. "Garden palette... of a painter crazy about flowers", is how Giverny looked to a writer of our times who was invite to the inauguration of the Fondation Claude Monet. Giverny is a living museum where the strolling visitor can see the abundantly flowered paths from which Monet drew his material, and dream of the fusion of reality with an inner vision, which was the hallmark of his work "A painter of light", as his friend Clémenceau said.

"... I do not know Mr. Monet.
I do not even think that I have ever
carefully looked at one of his paintings.
Yet I feel as though I am one of his oldest friends.
That is because his painting tells me a tale of energy and truth...
We have more than a realist here, we have a delicate and
powerful interpreter who knows how to render each detail
without falling into dryness." ZOLA

Claude Monet
"Les Roses" - Detail
1925-1926 - Oil on canvas
130 x 200 cm.
Musée Marmottan, Paris.

the changing light. He was obsessed and tortured by his painting. He painted furiously and, very often dissatisfied, destroyed his work. When in such a mood, his family created an atmosphere of respectful silence around him. But when a painting was successful, he once more became cheerful, approachable and the most pleasant man in the world.

He would rise at five o'clock each morning and wander along the paths of Giverny, the banks of the river Epte and the rows of poplars, in the fields red with poppies and along the banks of the Seine. It was at Giverny that he became the forerunner of modern painting. Disregarding all the tendencies of his time, the Nabis, Pointillists, Fauvists and Cubists, he followed his own furrow. "The subject is of secondary importance to me; what I want to reproduce is what exists between the subject and me". "The subject of his painting is not light and shade, but the painting placed in light and shade". In this way, the subject

to Georges Durand-Ruel
on June 3, 1905:
... Are the colors I use
as interesting as
all that? I don't think so,
considering that
you can achieve more
brightness with any
other palette. The main
thing is to know how to
use colors, the choice of
which boils down to a
matter of habit.
MONET

disappeared from his paintings at the end of his life, thus heralding the arrival of abstract art.

It was at Giverny that he began his well-known "Séries" which later made him famous. He painted the series of twenty-five "Haystacks" between 1888 and 1891. In 1892, he exhibited a set of twenty-four Poplars at the Durand-Ruel gallery; from 1892 to 1898, he painted the series of Cathedrals, "Matinées sur la Seine" and then the Japanese Bridge, Wistarias and Water Lilies with their interplay of sky, clouds, grass and flowers. All is reflected on a surface which is itself illusory. And finally came the apotheosis with the large decorative panels of water lilies, called the "Décorations des Nymphéas", in which shapes gradually

"Claude Monet handles light waves like the musician does sound waves. The two kinds of vibrations are related to each other. Their harmonies obey the same inescapable laws. Two tones juxtaposed in a painting follow rules that are as strict as those governing two notes in harmony.
Even better: the different episodes of a series follow each other like the different parts of a symphony. Pictorial drama grows according to the same principals as musical drama."
GRAPPE

Opposite : Claude Monet "La Maison de l'Artiste vue du Jardin aux Roses" 1922-1924 - Oil on canvas 89 x 92 cm.
Musée Marmottan, Paris.

Left: Monet
In front the Japanese bridge

give way to a triumph of colour.

At the time of his move to Giverny he was in dire financial straits and the art dealer Durand-Ruel, through his financial support, helped Monet and his large family to live comfortably. As he became more widely known and his canvases began to sell well, Monet decided to buy the house for the sum of 22,000 francs. He then altered the garden, constructed three greenhouses and, on the other side of the "chemin du Roy", bought a plot of land on which, after countless administrative difficulties, he succeeded, in 1895, in creating the famous pond and built the Japanese Bridge after an engraving. In 1892, he married Alice Hoschedé who, respected and respectable, brought an element of stability into his life. Cézanne, Renoir, Sisley, Pissarro, Matisse, John Singer Sargent, the critic Gustave Geffroy and Octave Mirbeau

"I want to paint the air in which the bridge, the house and the boat lie. The beauty of the air in which they are, and that is nothing other than impossible." MONET

After moving to Giverny, Claude Monet strove to follow the subtle effects of the sun's course the same subject's variations in light as the hours and seasons go by. In the series, the main subject is not the landscape itself but its changing luminosity and color.

visited him there. He became an intimate friend of Georges Clemenceau, who showered him with admiration and affection until his death. He neither understood nor could bear Gauguin's painting but liked that of Vuillard – "a very good eye" – and Maurice Denis – "a very fine talent". After lunch, he liked showing his friends his private collection on the first floor of his house. In 1899, he had a second studio built for its particularly good light, to the left of the garden, in front of the greenhouses. He also had a garage constructed as well as a dark room for photography and two bedrooms. During this period, art dealers vied with each other for his clientele. He entrusted his canvases to Boussod and Valadon, to the Bernheim brothers and to Georges Petit, and Durand-Ruel suffered cruelly because of this. However, it was at the latter's gallery that he exhibited a magnificent series of Water Lilies (1900) and became famous throughout France, England and the United States.

In 1899, too, his daughter-in-law, Suzanne, died, an irreparable loss for her mother.

Exhibitions and trips to Norway, London, Italy and the Normandy coast followed in rapid succession.

In May 1911, the death of his wife left him completely at a loss. Fortunately, he still had his daughter-in-law, Blanche, and Georges Clemenceau.

His son, Jean, Blanche's husband, died in 1914. Completely shattered, Monet began to suffer from cataracts; Clemenceau urged him to press on with his artistic research. He therefore began to dream of creating the "Décorations des Nymphéas", for which he built a huge and unsightly studio from 1914 to 1915, at the top of the garden, on the left. His gigantic task was begun in 1916 and, after various ups and downs, ended with a magnificent series of canvases being donated to France on 12th April 1922.

In January and July 1923, he underwent operations on his right eye. He died depressed and exhausted on 5th December 1926.

Michel Monet, his second son, with whom relations had been strained, was his father's heir. He lived in Sorel, Eure-et-Loir, but occasionally came to Giverny, where everything had remained as it was, devotedly watched over by his sister-in-law, Blanche. She looked after the property and gardens and kept alive the memory of the master until her death after the Second World War. The head gardener,

Lebret, also died and the care of the property was left to an assistant gardener. Gradually, the garden fell into neglect, most of the paintings were sold and, on returning from a visit to Giverny, Michel, then aged 88, was injured in a car accident and died on 19 January 1966.

In his will, Michel left the entire property to the Académie des Beaux-Arts. Appointed Curator of Giverny by my colleagues in 1977, I immediately undertook the preservation of the gardens, with the help of funds from the Institut and donations from the Conseil Général de l'Eure, the Préfecture de l'Eure and the Association "Richesses de l'Eure".

I then took on a head gardener, M. Vahé, a brilliant student

The little bridge across the creek flowing from the Epte appears through the azalea bushes lining the north bank of the pond.

His goal was to record, develop and fix the memories specific to a chosen place, to the changing seasons, hours, weather, climate, light, heat and color, changes having to do with the course of a single day. GURALNIK

The studio located at the north-west corner of the grounds is where the master showed his unfinished works to art dealers and filled in their borders once they were sold. Today the studio contains the glassed-in bookcases where Monet's newly rebound and catalogued books can be seen. Many of them are dedicated. Many are on cooking and botany.

*"After walking through the garden composed like a palette,
where the flower banks are arranged in bright, magical tones,
where the eye is dazzled by so many different living colors, this
decorative vision is restful. The whole setting at Giverny is an atmospher
that the painter has arranged for himself, and living there makes
an ongoing contribution to his work. During his leisure time
- sometimes he does nothing for month - he carries on with his work
without seeming to, simply by taking walks.
His eye contemplates, study, stores...
His studio is nature."* GUILLEMOT

from the Ecole Nationale d'Horticulture. Georges Truffaut, whom the master invited to dine with him, often visited him at Giverny.

He was accompanied by a young man, M. André Devillers, who later became general manager of the Georges Truffaut Company. With the help of M. Thibaudin, he was kind enough to give me the benefit of his experience and memories. I am also greatly indebted to M. Toulgouat (Claude Monet's great-nephew) and his wife for a long and detailed study of a theoretical reconstitution of the gardens. Finally, André de Vilmorin kindly helped me with his expert opinion. Let me express my thanks to all these people. Through them, and the work and talent of M. Vahé, a miracle has taken place : the garden is at last back to its original state.

Once the funds donated by the Institut were depleted, my wife (an American, and President of the Versailles Foundation)

and I left for the United States where we were authorized to accept tax-deductible donations for Giverny from Americans through the Versailles Foundation.

A great friend of France and a fervent admirer of Claude Monet, Mrs. Lila Acheson Wallace, generously made a very important donation.

Other friends from New York, Washington, Chicago, Palm Beach, New Orleans, Dallas, Houston, Los Angeles, San Francisco and naturally, from France, also offered us their financial support. Ambas-sador Walter Annenberg spontaneously gave a large sum to connect the gardens and ponds with a tunnel (under the new road which has, alas, replaced the former "chemin du Roy"). This way, although

The long-neglected mauve wisteria once again soars towards the rebuilt Japanese bridge.

"... With you it's another matter. The steel ray of your eye shatters the outer shell of appearances and you penetrate the profound substance, decomposing it into vehicles of light that you recompose with your brush. As vigorously as possible you re-establish the effect of sensations on the surfaces of our retinas. And whereas when I look at a tree I see nothing more than a tree, you, with half-closed eyes, think, 'How many tones of how many colors can be found in the luminous transitions of this single stem?'"
CLEMENCEAU

the two parts of the property remain separate, visitors can go straight from one to the other. Each year the Claude Monet Foundation welcomes many visitors from all over the world.

As Claude Monet's fame spread, American painters gradually moved to Giverny from 1890 onwards.

The first of these was Theodore Robinson, introduced to

**Claude Monet
"Nymphéas. Effet du Soir"
1897-1898 - Oil on canvas
73 x 100 cm. Detail.
Musée Marmottan, Paris.**

**Claude Monet
"Nymphéas"
1903 - Oil on canvas
73 x 92 cm.
Musée Marmottan, Paris.**

Claude Monet by a friend; he moved from Fontainebleau to settle at Giverny.

Another American artist, Metcalf, moved into an inn called "L'Auberge Baudy" and was invited to dinner by Claude Monet.

Then came the invasion which drove Monet to despair : the Belgian, Théo van Rysselberghe, William Hart, Miss Wheeler, the Czech, Radinsky, the Norwegian, Thornley, the Scot, Watson, the Americans, Beckwith, Theodore Butler, Johnstone, Finn, Perry and Lila Cabott Peery, Hart Friescke, Mary Cassatt, Rosc, etc., and the inn became the "Hôtel Baudy". After Claude Monet's death, a number of surrealists also settled at Giverny.

Many abstract painters have spoken of the influence of Monet's last canvases on their own work. For them, the

If he dared,
a philosopher dreaming
before a water painting
by Monet would develop
the dialectics of the iris
and water lily,
the dialectics of the
straight leaf and the leaf
that is calmly,
peacefully, heavily lying
on the water's surface.
This is the very dialectic
of the aquatic plant.
Reacting to some kind of
spirit of revolt, the one
wants to spring up
against its native
element. The other is
loyal to its element. The
water lily has understood
the lesson of calm taught
by still waters. With such
a dialectical dream, one
might feel the soft,
extremely delicate
verticality that can be
seen in the life of still
waters. But the painter
feels all that instinctively
and knows how to find in
the reflections a sure
principal that makes up,
vertically, the peaceful
world of water.
BACHELARD

Claude Monet
"Nymphéas"
1916-1919 - Oil on canvas
200 x 180 cm.
Musée Marmottan, Paris.

Until then I knew
only naturalist and,
to tell the truth,
almost exclusively
Russian naturalist art... I
believed that no one
had the right to paint
so imprecisely.
I vaguely felt that the
object (the subject) was
missing in this work.
But with astonishment
and confusion,
I observed that not
only did it surprise,
but it imprinted itself
indelibly in the
memory and that
before your eyes
it recomposed itself
in the smallest details.
All this remained
muddled in me, and I
could not yet
foresee the
natural consequences
of this discovery.
But what clearly
came out of it
is the incredible power,
a power I had never
known, of a palette
that outstripped my
wildest dreams.
To me the painter
seemed gifted with a
fabulous power. The
Object used as an
indispensable element in
my work unconsciously
lost some of its
importance to me.
In short, there was
already a little bit
of my enchanting
Moscow on this
canvas." KANDINSKY

"Water Lilies" are not minor decorative "post-impressionist" works but rather go a step beyond impressionism. They are a vertical interpretation of a horizontal scene — the surface of water — a rejection of all traditional limits. The interplay of reflections alone recreates all the surrounding nature, the colours explode to the detriment of all figurative form. "They gave to painting a fantastic strength and brilliance. But, unconsciously, the object, as an indispensable element of a painting, was also discredited", wrote Kandinsky. However, one should also quote André Masson and Joan Mitchell and recognize Monet's influence in the paintings of many contemporary artists, such as Pollock, Sam Francis, Judith Reigl, etc.

Claude Monet may thus be considered not only as one of the greatest painters of his time but also as a precursor of modern art.

"... This is where Monet came to refine his sensations, making them as sharp as possible. He would remain here in his armchair for hours without moving, without speaking, peering at the undersides of passing and sunlit things, trying to read in their reflections the elusive glimmer where mysteries are revealed. Speech is disdained to confront the silence of fleeting harmonies. Is not seeing understanding?...."

GEORGES CLEMENCEAU

Claude Monet
"Nymphéas"
1916 - 1919 - Oil on canvas
150 x 197 cm.
Musée Marmottan, Paris

Claude Monet
by Sacha Guitry

THE HOUSE GIVERNY

The house, too, has been restored. When the Académie des Beaux-Arts took over possession in 1966, the architect and member of the Académie, Jacques Carlu, was appointed curator. He immediately had the roof

The same harmonious cohesiveness between house and garden that existed when Monet lived here has been recreated.

The second studio, built in 1899, has been completely restored.

repaired but the interior was left without any heating due to lack of funds. In the wet climate, the furniture began to disintegrate, eaten away by fungus, the wainscoting, floors and ceiling beams rotted away, a staircase collapsed. The same happened in the second studio, opposite the greenhouses, and in the water lily studio, where tree shoots began to grow. Jacques Carlu had the master's forty-six canvases, left

Utamaro Kitagawa
(1753 - 1806)
"A Young Woman Combs
Her Hair and Feeds Her
Distracted Child"

The reconstructed dining
room.

by his son, moved to the Musée Marmottan, where they are displayed in new surroundings. The mildewed Japanese engravings, their frames eaten into by worms, were stored in chests. The china, ceramic vases and furniture remain, as does the copperware in the kitchen. Ten years passed before I was able, as curator of the Claude Monet Foundation, to undertake the entire restoration of all the buildings with the competent and dedicated help of Georges Luquiens, an architect from the Institut, thanks to Lila Achezson Wallace's donation and the wise and astute advice of her lawyer, William Barnabas McHenry.

The façade of the central building was renovated. With the pink of its crushed brick surface and its green doors and shutters, it strikingly resembles an impressionist painting of the last century. It was Claude Monet who chose this green for the seats and ironwork in his garden as well as for the doors, shutters and wood on

鶯

笹丹朱玲成

the terrace, where he often liked to sit after the evening meal.

The walls and furniture of the dining-room, to the right as one enters the house, have been repainted in their two slightly different shades of yellow. (This room was originally a small bedroom and kitchen). The dinner-service, of which the remaining pieces tone in with the colours in the dining room, was ordered from Limoges. The curtains have been rewoven, the same "China blue" decorates the glass-doored sideboards and the same Japanese engravings, cleaned, newly framed and identified hang in the same spots in this well-known room, remarkably full of life and memories. Claude Monet began his collection of Japanese engravings in 1871 and it could be said that he created the taste for things Japanese among the painters of his time.

His purchases show the most unerring taste; he particularly liked Utamoro, Hiroshige, Hokusaï, Toyokuni, Kiyonaga, Shunsho and Sharaku, whose works have been identified by the English art historian, David Bromfield. The generosity of Hélène David Weill made possible the restoration not only of the engravings but of all the furniture.

Claude Monet built an extension onto his house by using the site of a small barn for his kitchen. This room was also very dilapidated. Today it gleams with the brilliance of its blue and white tiles and its restored and newly tinned copper. The stove (which does not work)

Above: Hiroshige Utagawa
(1797 - 1868)
"The rice paddies of Asakusa during the festival of the rooster"

Opposite:
Utamaro Kitagawa
(1753 - 1806)
"Owl on a tree trunk and two robins".

Chikanobu Yōshu
(1838 - 1912)
"Awabi Divers Plunging
into the Sea in the
Province of Sgami".

The kitchen'soriginal
earthenware and copper
utensils restored.

*"It is true that at Giverny Monet is always
a little in Japan. He lives in the company of landscapes by
Hiroshiga and Hokusai, which probably fulfill some
of his desire to travel, assuming he feels any.
Having lunch in front of The Road from Kiso, leafing through a magazine
in the mauve sitting room in the company of The Wave or passing
Western Ships in Yokohama Harbor or The Twin Rocks
on the way to the studio-sitting room
is his everyday way of travelling."* JOYES

has been restored to look as it originally did, the sink, scales and weights and the sewing-machine are all there to evoke vividly middle-class life in the country at the end of the 19th century.

One of the most interesting features of the Claude Monet Foundation is the artist's collection of Japanese engravings. In addition to the dining room and drawing room on the ground floor, several rooms on the second floor have been set aside for this collection which will no doubt make up a fascinating discovery for many visitors.

To the left of the front door, opposite the dining room, is a small reading room with its authentic furniture restored; this room opens onto a second entrance, often used by Claude Monet to go up to his bedroom or to sit in his studio, which he also used as a sitting room after each meal.

This room (like his bedroom on the first floor) was created on the site of a single-storey barn with a mud floor. Here, too, the past is evoked with striking authenticity, the very simple furniture is there, from his easel, cane chairs and his sofa with its sleeping china cat (a gift from Pierre Sicard), to the hemp carpet, cleaned and renewed.

On the walls, Claude Monet hung his canvases in three rows. Gérard Delorme has generously made a gift of these paintings, identical replicas of the master's works, created by means of his new process of reproduction in colour and relief. They bring life and vitality to the walls of this studio.

On the floor above the studio is the master's bedroom; it was here that he slept from 1883 to 1926; here, too, that he died. All the furniture still exists, including a superb 18th century marquetry writing-desk and a very fine antique chest of drawers. The fabrics on the walls and armchairs have been rewoven. Beside this room is his washroom, that of Alice his wife, and her bedroom. On the other side of the central staircase were the children's bedrooms and, in the attic, those of the servants. It was in his bedroom and the adjoining rooms

Kunisada Utagawa
(1780 - 1865)
"The Awabi Divers".

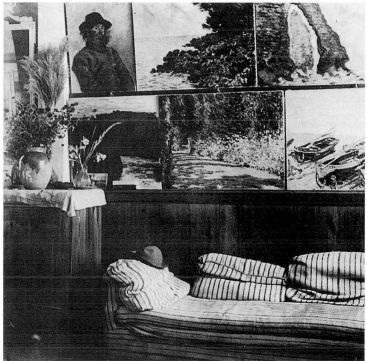

that Claude Monet kept the collection that he liked to show his friends. It was here, too, that he hung the paintings he had bought from or had been given by painters whose talent he held in esteem. Among them were twelve Cézannes, including "Le Nègre Scipion", a portrait of Claude Monet and his wife, another portrait of Madame Monet reading "Le Figaro", two nudes and "The Kasbah of Algiers", all by Renoir; eight Manets, five Berthe Morisots, two Degas, three Delacroix, a Fantin-Latour, several Pissarros, a Signac, a Vuillard, "Rain", by Caillebotte, four Jongkinds, two Rodin bronzes...

A magnificent collection now scattered throughout various museums in all parts of the world.

The sitting room-studio in
the west corner.

to Geffroy on March 28, 1893
"... and I tell myself that whoever says he has finished a painting
is terribly arrogant. Finished means complete, perfect, and I
am working hard without moving ahead, searching, feeling my way
without achieving much..."
MONET

The bedroom of Claude
Monet's wife, Alice

Utamaro Kitagawa
(1753 - 1806)
"A mother watching over
her playing child".

Left:
Claude Monet's
bedroom

THE CLOS NORMAND

The Clos Normand is designed in the French style. It lies in front of the house, intersected by paths running in straight lines, and is ordered despite the profusion, variety and brilliance of the colours which change with the seasons. Claude Monet's love of gardening was enhanced through his friendship with Caillebotte, at Argenteuil. Wherever he lived, he had a small garden, at Ville d'Avray, Louveciennes, Argenteuil and Vétheuil.

No exhibition focusing on Monet's Giverny can present the paintings in a purely abstract context. It must also take account of how the garden itself is intertwined with the texture of each work. This garden is one of Monet's masterpieces. He designed every aspect of it before turning its actual landscaping over to a team of specialists. His paintings have made this garden immortal. The layout of the flower-beds, paths, water lily pond and footbridge is no more the fruit of chance than the many striking juxtapositions of colors and wide brush strokes of the late paintings in which they appear.

PH. DE MONTEBELLO

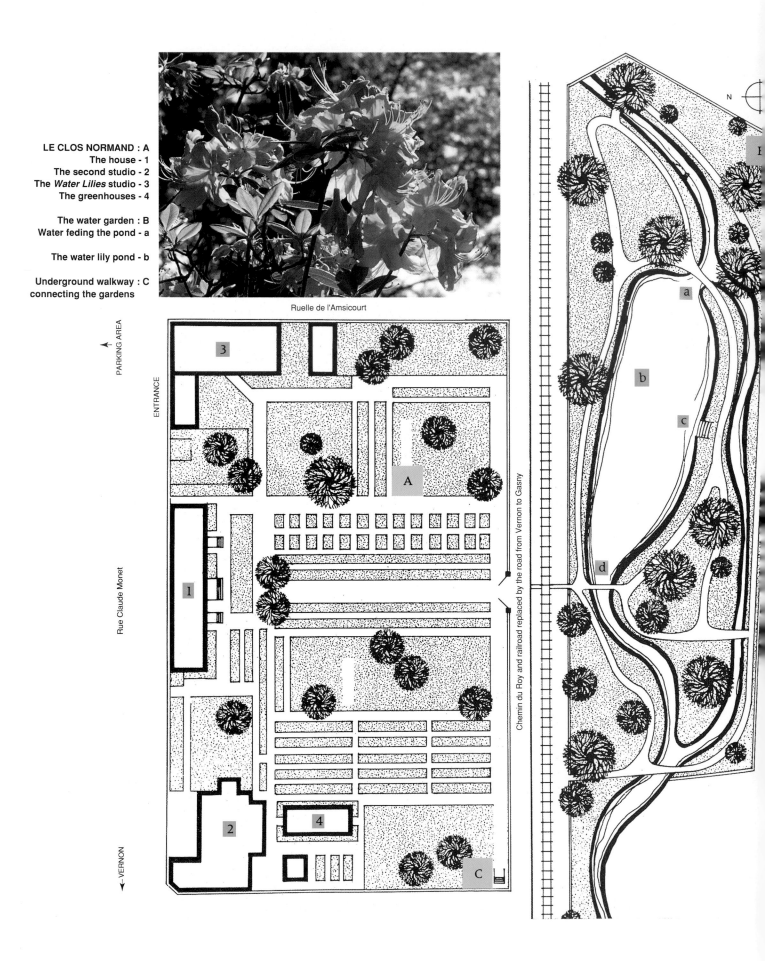

LE CLOS NORMAND : A
The house - 1
The second studio - 2
The *Water Lilies* studio - 3
The greenhouses - 4

The water garden : B
Water feding the pond - a

The water lily pond - b

Underground walkway : C
connecting the gardens

Ruelle de l'Amsicourt

PARKING AREA

ENTRANCE

Rue Claude Monet

← VERNON

Chemin du Roy and railroad replaced by the road from Vernon to Gasny

N

At Giverny, he at last owned an orchard, through the middle of which ran a large pathway flanked by two wide flower beds and ending at the "chemin du Roy". In the flowerbeds grew spruces, yew trees and large clumps of box tree. After endless painful arguments with Alice, he kept the two yews in front of the house and replaced the spruces and box trees with metal archways and, under the arcade of roses, the central pathway was lined with flowers and creeping nasturtiums. His head gardener was the son of Octave Mirbeau's gardener, Felix Breuil who had five assistants to help him.
On the west side, he transformed the orchard into lawns dotted with clusters of irises and Oriental poppies and Japanese cherry and apple trees.

Georges Clémenceau said about his friend Claude Monet, "his garden was his studio." Indeed, the painter was lovingly attached to it.

"... Like everyone else, I have already noticed that at the distance Monet necessarily places himself to paint, the onlooker can make out nothing but a storm of furiously blended colors on the canvas. A few steps back and on the same canvas he sees nature reshaped and miraculously arranged through an inextricable tangle of multi-colored spots that disconcert us at first sight. A prestigious symphony of tones follows the web of mixed colors. How could Monet, who did not move, grasp, from the same viewpoint, the decomposition and recomposition of the tones that enabled him to achieve the desired effect? ...." CLEMENCEAU

He had regular strips of gladioli, lark-spur, phlox, daisies, asters, etc. planted on the east side. A metal trellis along each strip was crowned with a sumptuous drapery of clematis undulating in the wind and edged a little lower down with climbing roses. The effect was delightful. The borders were adorned with rockery plants, with blue the dominant colour, and the annuals alternated with the perennials so that there were constantly some plants in flower.

At last I have found wallflowers. There are good gardeners here. Several packages will arrive in Vernon. They must be carefully unwrapped. There will be other plants, perennial plants, and also passion-flowers for the temperate greenhouse as well as two very pretty yellow flowers and two odd little nasturtiums."
MONET A ALICE HOSCHEDE

Claude Monet
"L'Allée des Rosiers.
Giverny"
1920-1922 - Oil on canvas
89 x 100 cm.
Musée Marmottan, Paris.

Right page:
Monet on the Rosebush
path

"They're bringing them
to me one after
the other. A color
that I had found and
sketched on one
of these canvases
yesterday reappears in
the air. I am quickly
given this painting and
strive to fix this vision
as permanently as
possible. But it usually
vanishes as fast as it
sprang up, making way
for another color I had
already painted days
ago on another
study instantly put in
front of me... and that is
the way it is
all day long..."
MONET

Naturally, the garden changed colour each season. In spring, it was filled with narcissi followed by tulips, azaleas, rhododendrons, lilacs and wistarias and the irises which Monet loved particularly and planted in long, wide rows. Then came the tree or herbaceous peonies, gifts from

his Japanese friends, followed by bellflowers, varieties of lilies, delphiniums, lupins and poppies.

In June, with the summer, came morning glories, sweet peas, bellflowers, blanket flowers, snapdragons, rose trees in all their varieties, stocks, columbines, foxgloves, nasturtiums, phlox, gentians, sage...

September brought both single and cactus dahlias, Japanese anemones, various kinds of sunflowers, hollyhocks and asters by the hundreds...

"As for the rest, what does form matter? What does the subject matter? What does the very landscape one wants to paint matter? What do all these elements, these fantastic, endlessly clashing shapes matter? Mr. Monet knows well that the only real thing is light. He knows that without it, everything would be shadow, everything would remain in a chaotic night. Light is all-powerful, it magnifies forms, makes them look beautiful, renews their vividness, transforms their appearances, moves their outlines and breathes life into them. Light is what populates the universe with imponderable atoms, it is the adornment of an eternally renewed poetry." GRAPPE

Claude Monet
"Iris jaunes et mauves
1924-1925 - Oil on canvas
106 x 155 cm.
Musée Marmottan, Paris.

In the three greenhouses, Monet cultivated climbing begonias, exotic ferns and a superb collection of orchids. "After seeing Claude Monet in his garden", said Kahn in 1904, "one can understand better how a gardener of such quality became such a great painter". And Claude Monet used to say of himself : "I am good for nothing except painting and gardening".

Right:
Monet touching up
the borders of
a painting in the studio.

THE WATER GARDEN

"Man is absent yet
entirely in the
landscape..." CEZANNE

Most often, the strolling
visitor can make out the
water garden's various
aspects through short
perspectives, but this
depth sometimes
disappears, as it does
in the painter's works
and, partially, in reality
itself. Claude Monet
achieved his goal of
having the effects
of light predominate in
the burgeoning
vegetation on the banks
ot the pond.
The softly-shaped
flowers are spots of
color offorod up to tho
moving air in which
light and shadow
incessantly play with
each other.

In 1893, Claude Monet bought a plot of land separated from the "Clos Normand" by the little railroad and the "chemin du Roy".
After a great many complicated administrative dealings, he was finally able to have the ponds dug.
Although the two sections of the property remain separate, an underpass enables visitors to wander

Above:
Claude Monet
"Le Bassin des Nymphéas"
"Harmonie verte"
1899 - Oil on canvas
80 x 60 cm.
Musée d'Orsay, Paris.

Opposite:
Claude Monet
"La Barque"
1887 - Oil on canvas
146 x 133 cm.
Musée Marmottan, Paris.

"... The effect varies unceasingly. Not only from one season to another but from one minute to the next, because the water lilies are far from being the only thing in the show; as a matter of fact, they are merely the accompaniment. The motif's essential is the mirror of water whose aspect is constantly being modified by the changing sky reflected in it, and which imbues it with life and movement. The passing cloud, the cooling breeze, the sudden storm that threatens to burst and finally does, the wind that stirs and suddenly blows with full force, the light that fades and is reborn are all things, elusive to the eyes of the uninitiated, that transfigure the color and shape of the bodies of water." MONET

Claude Monet
"Le Pont Japonais"
1918-1919 - Oil on canvas
74 x 92 cm.
Musée Marmottan, Paris.

"I have undertaken things that are impossible to do. Water with grass waving beneath its surface... it is beautiful to see, but wanting to paint that is enough to drive you crazy. Those are the kinds of things I always try to tackle!" MONET

"... I see nothing but a successful transposition of cosmic realities, such as modern science has revealed them to us, in this `dusty haze' of things Monet encounters at the end of his brush. I do not claim that Monet has reproduced the atoms' dance. I am simply saying that he has taken a big step towards the emotive representation of the world and its elements by distributing light that corresponds to the vibrating waves which science has discovered. Can we change our current conception of the atom? Monet's genius will have made us make incomparable progress in our perceptions of the world, which must always be taken into account whatever the future of our knowledge..."
CLEMENCEAU

Right page:
Claude Monet
"Le Pont Japonais"
1918-1924 - Oil on canvas
89 x 100 cm.
Musée Marmottan, Paris.

through the whole estate. The Japanese Bridge, reconstructed today, was built in 1895.

In the review, "Jardinage", 1924, Georges Truffaut described this water garden as it was in all its splendour. "The pond, whose water comes from the river Epte, is surrounded by weeping willows with golden boughs. The bed and banks are filled with a mass of plants such as heather, ferns, laurel, rhododendrons, azaleas and holly. The water's edges are shaded on one side by the abundant foliage of roses-trees and in the pond itself grows every known variety of water lily. On the banks, irises of several varieties

Claude Monet
"Le Pont Japonais"
1918-1924 - Oil on canvas
89 x 100 cm.
Musée Marmottan, Paris.

are thrown into relief by tree peonies, Japanese and herbaceous peonies, clumps of laburnum and Judea trees. A large plantation of bamboos forms a thick wood. The banks also contain winter heliotropes with huge leaves on lawns of thalictrums with serrated leaves, certain kinds of ferns with light, downy, pink or white flowers and wistarias. There are also tamarisks and the whole garden is studded with rose trees and rosebushes.

Unlike the "Clos Normand", the Water Garden is Japanese in style, asymmetrical, exotic, and lends itself to reverie in the eastern tradition of the philosophical

"... This is where Monet came to refine his sensations, making them as sharp as possible. He would remain here in his armchair for hours without moving, without speaking, peering at the undersides of passing, sunlit things, trying to read in their reflections the elusive glimmer where mysteries are revealed. Speech's disdain for confronting the silence of fleeting harmonies. Is not seeing understanding?..."
CLEMENCEAU

"... at night I am obsessed with what I am striving to achieve. In the morning I get up broken by fatigue. The dawn gives me courage, but my anxiety rushes back as soon as I set foot into the studio. How difficult It Is to paint... It really Is torture. Last autumn I burned six paintings with the dead leaves from my garden. It is enough to make you lose all hope, yct I would not want to die without having said everything I have to say, or at least tried to say. And my days are numbered... Who knows what tomorrow will bring..." MONET

contemplation of nature. It was a crucial factor in the work of Claude Monet.

Throughout his life, he would often return there to dream, inspired by the subtle interplay of light and water. It was there that he painted his first sets of Water Lilies which formed the basis of the magnificent canvases created at the very end of his life, the famous "Décorations". These complete the cycle of this genius's work and clearly announce the whole

"It took me some time to understand my water lilies... I had planted them for the pleasure of it; I grew them without thinking of painting them... A landscape takes longer than a day to imbue you... And then, all of a sudden, I had the revelation of how magical my pond is. I took my palette. Since then I have scarcely had any other model." MONET

THE WATER LILY STUDIO

movement of abstract art, as Kandinsky so rightly pointed out.

It was built in 1916 (on the site of a tumbledown cottage) so that Monet could paint at ease and in good light the great "Décorations des Nymphéas", the finest set of which the master gave to France in 1922 at Georges Clemenceau's instigation. This is therefore the cradle of his artistic legacy. In very bad condition, this studio was restored at great expense thanks to Michel David Weill's two generous donations. The easels, several mobile trestles and the sofa are still here, and the walls are decorated with magnificent reproductions, gifts from Gérard Delorme, of Monet's large format paintings.

Claude Monet in the *Water Lilies* studio.

The visitor will enter the everyday world of the master of Giverny, walking through the huge *Water Lilies* studio bathed by the light in which *Décorations* was created. Most of the large paintings of the water garden were not done on the banks of the pond, but in this studio.

CLAUDE MONET FOUNDATION

BIBLIOGRAPHY
Our references for this work
include:
Arsène Alexandre : «Le jardin de
Monet»
Le Figaro, August 9, 1901
Maurice Kahn : «Le jardin de
Claude Monet»
Le Temps, June 7, 1904
Louis Vauxcelles : «Un après-midi
chez Claude Monet»
L'Art et les Artistes, May 15,
1909
Roger Marx : «Les Nymphéas de
M. Claude Monet»
La Gazette des Beaux-Arts,
1909
Gustave Geffroy :« Claude Monet,
sa vie, son temps, son œuvre»
Paris, 1912
Georges Truffaut : «Le jardin de
Claude Monet»
Jardinage 87, November 1924
Georges Clemenceau : «Claude
Monet - Les Nymphéas»
Paris, 1928
Jean-Pierre Hoschedé : «Claude
Monet ce mal connu»
Genève, 1960
René Gimpel : «Journal d'un
collectionneur, marchand
de tableaux»
Paris, 1963
Paulette Howard Johnston :
«Une visite à Giverny en 1924»
L'œil, March 1969
John Rewald : « The history of
Impressionism»
New York, 1973
Claire Joyes, «Monet at Giverny»
London, 1975
Daniel Wildenstein : «Monet's
years at Giverny - Beyond
Impressionism»
Metropolitan Mus. of Art, 1978

Thanks to Reader's Digest and to the Lila Wallace - Reader's Digest Fund, a farm consisting on three dilapited buildings and a plot of land located across the road from the House and Gardens of Claude Monet was purchased and the land converted into a parking lot, lined with trees and flowers.

The three buildings were rebuilt using the original stones. The building located directly on the Rue Claude Monet now houses the gardeners' headquarters, the Head Gardener's office and two rooms with kitchen and bathroom for volunteers.

In the right-hand building, thanks to donations, notably from Mr. Laurance Rockefeller, two appartments have been equipped to receive important donors who come to Giverny from time to time. Also thanks to Mr. Laurance Rockefeller, a flower shop and a cafeteria, decorated in the style of turn-of-the-century cafés with an adjoining garden across from the parking lot have been opened. Last but not least, the main building in the back of the courtyard has been fully restored by Reader's Digest. Three fully-equipped appartments and a large studio have been in use since 1988. Every year, Reader's Digest selects three American artists to come to Giverny to paint and visit the region. This is also a way of acknowledging the generosity of American donors without whom Giverny would not exist. Thanks to its friends in France, and, mostly, in the US, $14 million were collected of which every penny went to restore the buildings and the gardens of Claude Monet.

The *Académie des Beaux Arts* is well rewarded by the interest of visitors. In seven months, 400,000 people came to Giverny, which receives more visitors than any other site in Normandy.

The Giverny Donors

Lila Wallace - Reader's Digest Fund
L'Académie des Beaux-Arts
Le Conseil Général de l'Eure
La Société des Amis de Claude Monet
The Society of the Friends of the
Dallas Museum
The Society of the
Neuberger Museum
S.E. et Mrs Walter Annenberg
Mr and Mrs David B. Arnold, Jr.
Mrs Robert Arnold
Mrs Vincent Astor
Madame Léon Bazin
Mrs Leigh Block
Mrs Alfred Bloomingdale
Mr Patrick Burns
Mr and Mrs Edward Byron-Smith
Mr and Mrs Gardiner Cowles
Mrs Ethel Woodward de Croisset
Mrs Allerton Cushman
Monsieur et Madame Pierre David-Weill
Monsieur et Madame Michel David-Weill
The Ewind W. and Catherine M. Davis
Foundation
Mr and Mrs Frederick W. Davis
Monsieur et Madame Paul Desmarais
Deere and Company
Mrs Doris Duke
Mr and Mrs Charles Durand-Ruel
Mr and Mrs Thomas B. Evans Jr.
Comtesse Alain d'Eudeville
Mrs Charles Engelhard Jr.
Mrs Frank Jay Gould
The Florence J. Gould Foundation, Inc.
Mr Henry Ford II
Mr Alvin Fuller
Mr and Mrs David Granger
Mrs Dolly Green
Mr and Mrs Melville Hall
Mrs Ira Haupt
Mr and Mrs Jack Heinz
Mrs James Hooker
Mr and MrsPhilip Hulitar
Mr and Mrs George F. Jewet Jr.
Mrs Alistair J. Keith

Mrs Randolph Kidder
Mrs Eric Koenig
Mr and Mrs David L. Kreeger
Madame Yvonne Larsen
Mr and Mrs Joseph Lauder
Mr and Mrs Harding Lawrence
Mr and Mrs Irvin Levy
The Richard Lounsberry Foundation
Mrs Eugène McDermott
Mr and Mrs Robert Magowan
Madame Louis Marillonnet
Mr and Mrs Harris Masterson
Mr and Mrs Paul Mellon
S.E. et Madame Walter
Moreira Salles
Mrs Charles Munn
Mr Stavros Niarchos
Mr George Ohrstrom
Baron and Baroness Hubert von Pantz
Mr George Parker
Mrs Sandra Payson
Mr David Rockefeller
Mr Laurance Rockefeller
Baron Edmond de Rothschild
Mrs Madeleine Russell
Monsieur Henri Samuel
Mrs Jay Simmons
Mr Garrick O. Stephenson
Mr and Mrs Harold Stream
Mr and Mrs David Schiff
Marquise de Surian
Mr and Mrs Vernon Taylor Jr.
Miss Alice Tully
Monsieur et Madame Gerald Van der Kemp
Mr and Mrs William Vincent
Pierre J. Wertheimer Foundation
Mr and Mrs William Wood-Prince
Baroness van Zuylen
Bergdorf Goodman
Bloomingdale's
Ceramich Caleca, S.r.l.
Haviland and Parlon
Marshall Field's
Reed & Barton Corporation
West Point-Pepperell, Inc.

Editions ART LYS
Versailles
Lay-out : Aline Hudelot
Photographie credits:
Archives of the
Claude Monet Foundation
ART LYS/J. Girard
Erika Burnier
Musée Marmottan
R.M.N.
Photocomposition : ART LYS
Photoengraving : EFFE GRAPHIC
Printed on March 15, 2000
by Presses de Bretagne
Registered : April 2000
Copyright: EDITONS ART LYS
ISBN 2.85495.043.7

Cover page 4: Portrait of
Claude Monet -
Summer 26
Photo by Nickolas Avray

The following bodies are authorized to receive your donations:

Société des Amis de Claude Monet
Mr. Toulgouat, Chairman
Giverny
27620 GASNY

Versailles Foundation
Mrs. Van der Kemp
420, Lexington avenue
Graybar building NEW YORK CITY N.Y. 10170

The Claude Monet Foundation is open from 10 a.m. to 6 p.m., except on Mondays from April 1 to October 31.